McGraw-Hill Reading
Wonders

Mc Graw Hill Education

Bothell, WA • Chicago, IL • Columbus, OH • New York, NY

Cover and Title Pages: Nathan Love

www.mheonline.com/readingwonders

The *McGraw·Hill* Companies

 **Education**

Copyright © 2014 The McGraw-Hill Companies, Inc.

Send all inquiries to:
McGraw-Hill Education
Two Penn Plaza
New York, New York 10121

ISBN: 978-0-02-119530-5
MHID: 0-02-119530-7

Printed in the United States of America.

7 8 9 0 QVS 18 17 16 15 14

CCSS Reading/Language Arts Program

Program Authors

Diane August	Jan Hasbrouck
Donald R. Bear	Margaret Kilgo
Janice A. Dole	Jay McTighe
Jana Echevarria	Scott G. Paris
Douglas Fisher	Timothy Shanahan
David Francis	Josefina V. Tinajero
Vicki Gibson	

Education

Bothell, WA • Chicago, IL • Columbus, OH • New York, NY

THE BIG CONCEPT

Getting to Know Us

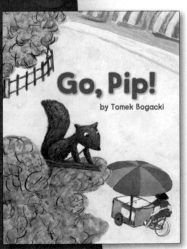

Go Digital! http://connected.mcgraw-hill.com/

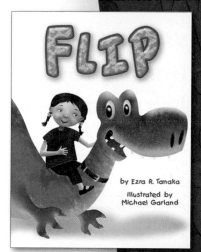
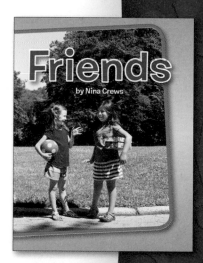

CCSS **Genre** Realistic Fiction

Essential Question

What do you do at your school?

Read about a boy who brings a special friend to school.

Go Digital!

6

Nat and Sam

by Pat Cummings

Nat is at **school**.

Nat sat.

What does Nat have?

Nat has Sam.

Nat does **not** have Sam!

Sam sat.

Sam is with Pam.

Look! Sam can read.

Can Nat? Nat can.

Nat and Sam like school.

Meet Pat Cummings

Pat Cummings moved a lot when she was growing up, so she understands why Nat would bring an old friend to a new place. She loves to draw and write stories. And like Nat and Sam, she loves to read a good book.

Author's Purpose

Pat Cummings wanted to tell a story about a boy and the things he does at school. Draw a picture of something you do at school.

Cats

©Marvin Lee

18

Respond to Reading

Retell

Use your own words to retell the important details in *Nat and Sam*.

Detail	Detail	Detail

Text Evidence

1. What happens to Sam after Nat brings him to school? **Key Details**

2. What details tell you why Nat and Sam like school? **Key Details**

3. How can you tell that *Nat and Sam* is realistic fiction? **Genre**

 Make Connections

What does Nat do that you can do at school, too?

Essential Question

Compare Texts
Read about how kids follow the rules at their school.

Rules at School

Our School Rules

Why do we have **rules** at school?

Rules can help us get along.
Rules can help us stay safe.

We raise our hands.

Stuart Pearce/Pixtal/age fotostock

We listen quietly.

We **obey safety** rules.

We let everyone play!
What are your school rules?

Make Connections

Why is it important to have rules at school? **Essential Question**

Essential Question

What is it like where you live?

Read about a squirrel's day out in the city.

Go Digital!

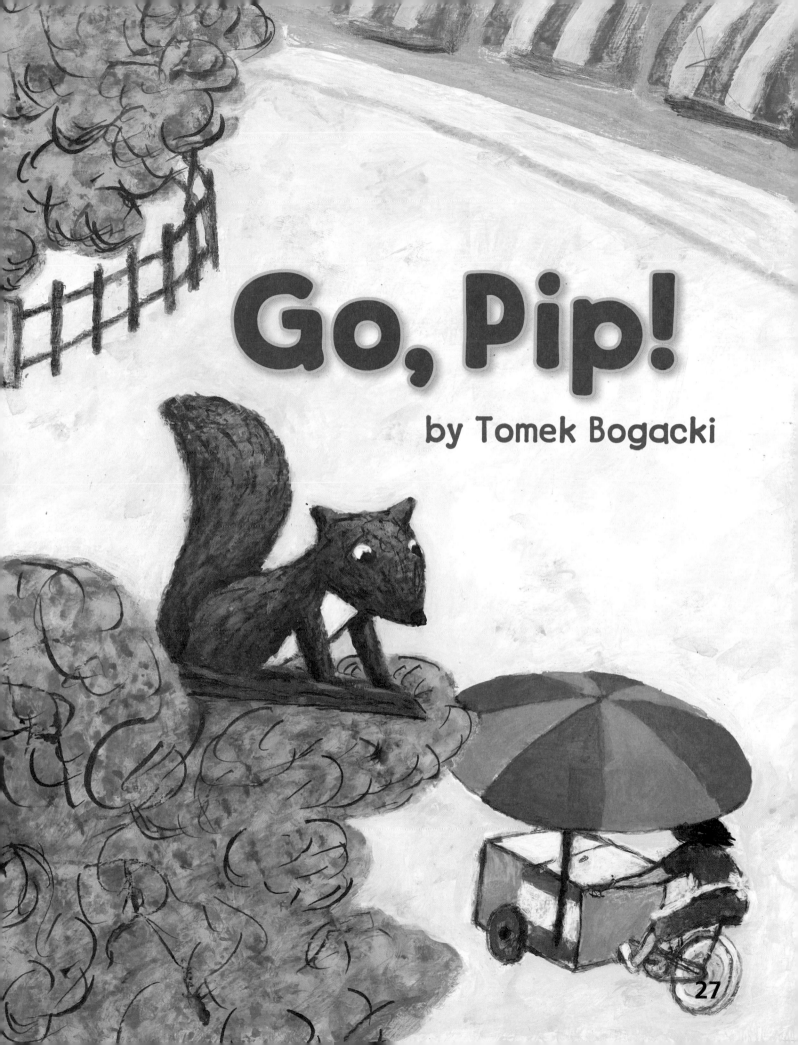

Go, Pip!

by Tomek Bogacki

Pip sits. Pip looks.

Pip can jump!

Pip is **out**.

Go, Pip!

Pip looks **up**.
It is **very** big.

Pip can look **down**.

Pip will go in.

Will this hat fit Pip?
It will!

Pip will go here.

Pip can look.

Where will Pip go?

Pip will go home!

Meet Tomek Bogacki

Tomek Bogacki used to live in a house in the forest. He liked to watch the animals there and draw pictures of them. Now he lives in a city where he likes to walk along the streets, visit museums, and watch squirrels in the park.

Author's Purpose

Tomek Bogacki wanted to tell a story about a curious squirrel who visits a city. Draw an animal visiting where you live. What might it see there?

Tomek Bogacki

Respond to Reading

Retell

Use your own words to retell the important details in *Go, Pip!*

Detail	Detail

Text Evidence

1. What details in the story and pictures tell you that Pip lives in a city? **Key Details**

2. What happens after Pip goes to the museum? **Key Details**

3. How can you tell that *Go, Pip!* is a fantasy? **Genre**

Make Connections
What other fun things could Pip do in a city? **Essential Question**

Compare Texts
Read about what it's like to live in the city or the country.

I Live Here

I live in the **country**.

I live in a house.

Not many people live near us.

I live in the **city**.
I live in a big **building**.
Lots of people live here.

I live in the **country**.
I play in my yard.
Lots of kids play with me.

I live in the **city**.
I play in the **playground**.
Lots of kids play with me.

I live in the **country**.
My school is far away.
I ride the bus.

I live in the **city**.
My school is near my home.
My mom walks with me.
Where do you live?

Make Connections

What might Pip do if he had a day out in the country?

Essential Question

Genre Fantasy

Essential Question

What makes a pet special?

Read about a very unusual pet who goes to school.

 Go Digital!

48

FLIP

by Ezra R. Tanaka

illustrated by
Michael Garland

Flip is my pet.
Flip is big.

Flip can not go in.
Flip is sad.

Flip **pulls** me in.

Flip and I go to class.

Flip sits.
Be good, Flip!

Flip likes class.

The kids like Flip.

Miss Black is mad.
Sit down, Flip!

Look at Miss Black!

Flip has a plan.

Flip did it!
The class claps.

Can Flip **come** back?
"Flip can," said Miss Black.
Flip is glad!

Meet the Illustrator

When **Michael Garland** was a child, he loved drawing characters from movies and books. Some of his favorite movies and books had funny creatures in them. So he drew a lot of dinosaurs just like Flip!

Illustrator's Purpose

Michael Garland likes to draw dinosaurs. Draw a dinosaur. Label your drawing.

Respond to Reading

Retell

Use your own words to retell three important details in *Flip*. Tell the details in order.

Detail	Detail	Detail

Text Evidence

1. What does Flip do when he gets to school? **Key Details**

2. What does Flip do to help Miss Black at the end? **Sequence**

3. How can you tell that *Flip* is a fantasy? **Genre**

Make Connections

How is Flip like the pets that you know? **Essential Question**

Compare Texts

Read about how to give pets what they need.

iguana

What Pets Need

What do pets **need**?

parrot

hamster

Like all **living things**, pets need food.
Some pets eat seeds or plants.

kittens

Some pets eat meat or fish.
All pets need fresh water.

dog

Pets need a safe home.
Pets need our love and **care**.

Make Connections

What do you think Flip needs? **Essential Question**

CCSS **Genre** Nonfiction

Essential Question

What do friends do together?

Read about how two friends have fun together.

Go Digital!

© Nina Crews

68

Friends

by Nina Crews

Pam and Jill are friends.
They play a lot.

Pam and Jill toss a ball.

Pam hops.
Jill hops, **too**!

They play tag.
Pam is quick.

Jill is not as quick as Pam.

Jill is hot.
She does not like tag.

© Nina Crews

Pam **makes** a plan.
She has a box.

Jill looks in.
It is a doll and a dog!

Pam and Jill sit on a rock.
They make up a game.

The dog and doll are friends.

Pam and Jill play, play, play.

It is a **fun** day!

Meet Nina Crews

Nina Crews uses photographs to tell stories about children. The children in the photographs are her family or friends. She says that her readers like to see pictures of real children.

Nina Crews

Author's Purpose

Nina Crews wanted to tell about real things friends do when they play together. Draw a picture of you and a friend playing.

Respond to Reading

Retell

Use your own words to retell three important details in *Friends*.

Detail	Detail	Detail

Text Evidence

1. What details tell you what Pam and Jill like to do? **Key Details**

2. What happens when Pam and Jill play tag? **Key Details**

3. How can you tell that *Friends* is nonfiction? **Genre**

Make Connections

What can friends do when they want to play different games?

Essential Question

There Are Days And There Are Days

by Beatrice Schenk de Regniers

There are days I want to be
all alone
with only me
for company—
me and my cat.
There <u>are</u> days like that.

84

And there are days
(many more)
I don't want to be alone
any more.
Then
it seems to me
jokes are funnier,
honey's honey-er,
sun is sunnier
when
I'm with a friend!

Make Connections
What does the boy like about being with a friend?
Essential Question

Illustration: Courtney A. Martin

85

Essential Question

How does your body move?

Read about the fun ways kids can move.

Go Digital!

Move It!

How can kids **move**?
We can move in lots of ways.
We use our bodies to help us.

86

I can **run**.
I have strong legs.
They help me go fast.

legs

feet

I can **jump**.
I pick up my feet.
I will land on the grass.

I can catch.
I use **two** hands.
I can grab the ball.

hands

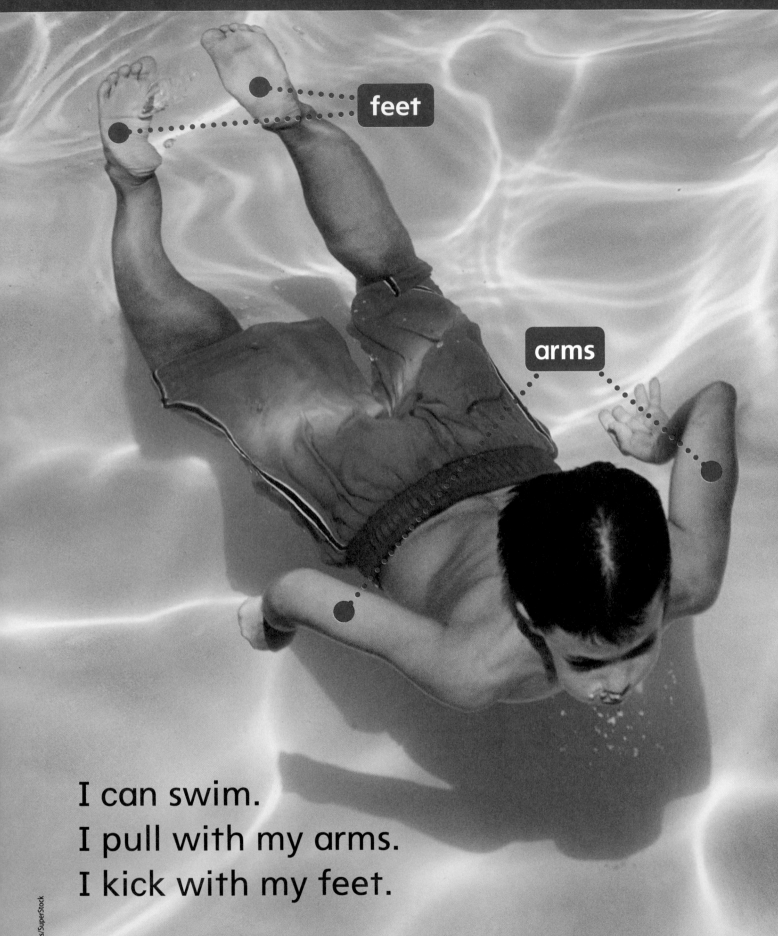

feet

arms

I can swim.
I pull with my arms.
I kick with my feet.

I can spin this hoop.
I move my hips fast.
This helps it stay up.

hips

I can do fun tricks.
There are lots of ways to move!
What can you do?

Respond to Reading

1. What body parts do kids use to swim? **Key Details**

2. What do the labels on each page tell you? **Key Details**

3. How can you tell that this is nonfiction? **Genre**

4. What else do your arms help you to do? **Essential Question**

Compare Texts

What body parts help kids move?

Using Diagrams

A diagram shows the different parts of something. It is a picture with labels. The labels name the parts.

Look at the fish and the girl. What parts do they both have that are the same?

fins

head

tail

gills

94

head

hand

shoulder

arm

leg

foot

Make Connections

What tricks do you think a fish could do with its body parts? **Essential Question**

Glossary

What is a Glossary? A glossary can help you find the meanings of words. The words are listed in alphabetical order. You can look up a word and read it in a sentence. Sometimes there is a picture to help you.

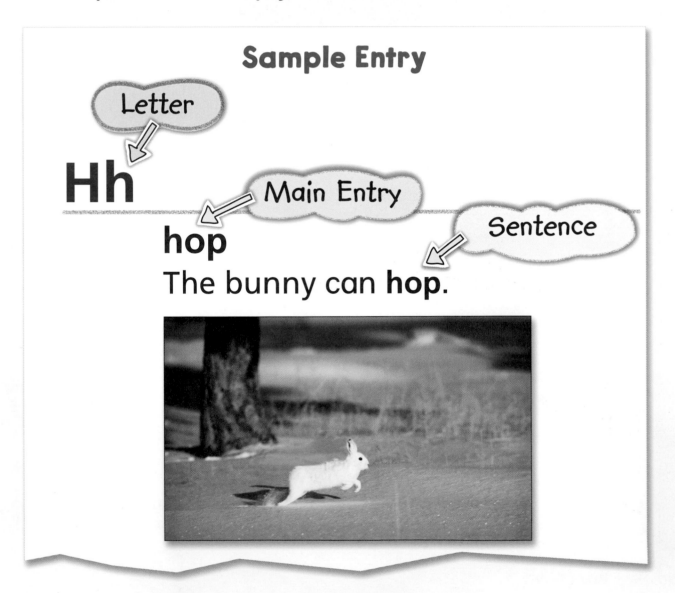

Sample Entry

Letter

Hh

Main Entry

hop

Sentence

The bunny can **hop**.

Bb

big

A hippo is **big**.

Cc

clap

Kim and Roz **clap**.

Dd

doll
I hug my **doll**.

Gg

good
This is **good** for me.

Hh

hat
This **hat** is red.

hop
The bunny can **hop**.

Mm

move
We **move** around and around.

Pp

pull
We **pull** on the rope.

Rr

run
It is fun to **run** in a race.

Ss

school
Our **school** is very big.

sit

The kids **sit** in a circle.

Tt

trick

We can see the **trick**.

two
Two kittens play.

Uu

up
The kite will go **up**.